TAKE THE SHOT

TOP GUN STRATEGIES FOR ACCELERATING, PROFIT, PRODUCTIVITY, AND PEACE OF MIND

BY ED RUSH

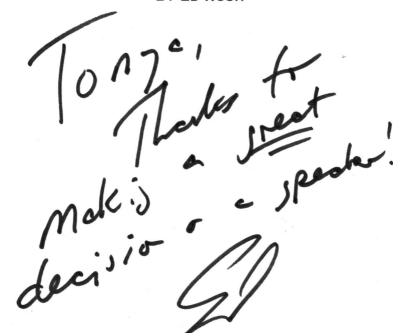

Take The Shot

Top Gun Strategies for Accelerating, Profit, Productivity, and Peace of Mind

By Ed Rush

"Twenty years from now you will be more disappointed by the things that you didn't do than by the ones you did do. So throw off the bowlines. Sail away from the safe harbor. Catch the trade winds in your sails. Explore. Dream. Discover."

- Mark Twain

Ed Rush & Associates, LLC
P.O. Box 1290
Bonita, CA 91908
619-292-2599
Fax: 619-292-2598
E-mail: Support@EdRush.com

Photos courtesy of: U.S. Department of Defense, Joint Strike Fighter Program Office.

Limits of Liability and Disclaimer of Warranty
The author and publisher shall not be liable for your misuse of this material. This book is for strictly informational and educational purposes.

Disclaimer
The views expressed are those of the author/Webmaster and do not reflect the official policy or position of the Department of Defense, the U.S. government, or the United States Marine Corps.

Copyright Use and Public Information
Unless otherwise noted, images have been used by permission and are in keeping with public information laws. Please contact the author for questions about copyrights or the use of public information.

General Information
Despite what you may have heard, there is no substantive proof that reading this book will make you more attractive to the opposite sex.

ABOUT THE AUTHOR

Anyone who has spent a significant amount of time in the cockpit of an F-18 fighter jet knows the value of *strategy* and the power of *focus*. Ed Rush is a speaker, a three-time #1 bestselling author, and a successful business consultant who has effectively taken the principles that he learned flying faster than the speed of sound and translated them into good business.

Ed has helped tens of thousands of event attendees and clients get more done in less time with less waste, not only giving clients the insights they need to grow, but gifting them with the power of *implementation* to change their businesses for better and for good.

Ed is a sought after speaker, bringing his dynamic gifts to the stage in engaging ways that make his clients look great. Ed also serves as the "secret weapon" that over 300 companies have brought in to help them increase profit & decrease waste, consulting them with honesty and effectiveness.

Ed's books and expertise have been featured on CBS, FOX, ABC, NBC, and in the *Opus Movie*. To book Ed to speak or for consulting, head over to: www.EdRush.com.

DEDICATION

This book is dedicated to my wife, Bonnie, whose advice is almost always right, yet rarely taken, and who never says, "I told you so."

Thanks for the good times.

Notably,

Starbucks, Japan, Horton, Morro Bay, Carmel, San Francisco, Topeka Place, Bristol, Kinsale, Paris, Napa, Troon Way...

and especially,

Yuma Regional, Sharp Memorial, and UCSD Medical Center where we first met Faith, Jack, and Dean.

CONTENTS

SECTION 1:

THE MAGIC MOVE

SECTION 1:

THE MAGIC MOVE

Curly: You know what the secret of life is?

Mitch: No, what?

Curly: This.

Mitch: Your finger?

Curly: One thing. Just one thing. You stick to that and everything else don't mean ****.

Mitch: That's great, but what's the one thing?

Curly: That's what you've got to figure out.

From the movie *City Slickers*

One thing you need to know is that we military folks use a lot of TLAs — that's Three-Letter Acronyms. Just between you and me, I don't think there is any other reason than because they sound cool.

Ready for a TLA?

For 7 years, I taught BFM. Impressed yet? Probably not. I get it.

BFM is Basic Fighter Maneuvering — the fundamentals of dogfighting. "BFM" is one plane against one plane. A young pilot cuts his teeth here before he moves on to bigger and better things like:

1 against 2

2 against 2

4 against 4

4 against 12

12 against 30

I've flown them all, and from experience I can tell you that there really is nothing better than a pure 1-on-1 BFM sortie. Oh, the adrenaline!

I will tell you about some of my favorite dogfighting stories in a few chapters, but for now, I want to tell you about a common characteristic in all young fighter pilots.

They all start out thinking that there is one magic move that will win all dogfights. They think that Maverick from Top Gun was right, and you really can 'just put on the brakes and let them fly on by.'

What our young padawan Jedi pilots soon learn is that true success comes in learning to play aerial chess. You outmaneuver your opponent one turn at a time, you wear him down, take advantage of his mistakes, and you don't make any mistakes yourself.

Having done that, you will soon find yourself moving behind him, and he will start looking backward at you. Once he starts looking back, you've got him nailed. (It's much harder to fly a plane looking backwards!)

Such is true in life, in business, in relationships — in everything. The truth is there are no magic moves, only consistent application of sound principles to move you forward.

The Japanese call this kaizen — the art of incremental self-improvement.

Fighter pilots call it training.

Whatever you call it, this book is about finding the fighter pilot inside you and changing your life for the better.

• If you want to be a more productive and successful person, you'll find the keys in this book.

• If you want to make more money and take more time off, keep reading.

• If you want to be a better leader, it's here.

• If you just want to hear some interesting stories, we've got that too.

A quick word about the length of this book — it is short for a reason!

I felt no compulsion to write War and Peace. You deserve better. In fact, the entire goal of this book is for you to be able to read it in one sitting and walk away ready to implement what you have learned.

To get the most out of this book, you only need to do three things:

1. Find a quiet place where you can read it without being interrupted by co-workers, employees, bosses, kids, e-mail, TV, radio, phone, or your receptionist. One hour should be enough.

2. Take notes right in this book. At least one page has been added at the end of each chapter for your notes. (If you write them anywhere else than in this book, they'll probably get lost.)

3. Be sure you leave each chapter with at least one action item. There is no sense in reading a book just for information. That'll only make you opinionated and poor. Decide on specific action items and set deadlines for accomplishing them.

Finally, when you are finished, be sure to shoot me a letter or an e-mail with your thoughts. I wrote this for you and I love hearing your success stories!

Have you found a quiet place yet?

Great! Let's get started.

SECTION 2:

INTO THE DARKNESS AND BACK AGAIN

What you can learn from trying

to land on a carrier...at night

Section 2:

Into the Darkness
and Back Again

"The whole world steps aside for the man who knows where he is going."

- Anonymous

"The first step to getting the things you want out of life is this: Decide what you want."

- Ben Stein

They call it "comfort time." I am not sure who came up with that definition, but in my humble opinion, it was anything but *comfortable*.

You see, there is a time in every Marine fighter pilot's life when he has to land on an aircraft carrier for the first time at night. Notice that I said "has to." The first night landing is anything but a good deal.

It is just about the most dangerous thing that I can ever remember doing. However, as a carrier pilot in the United States Marine Corps, I am proud to be a citizen in the only country that lands its aircraft on a carrier *at night* — crazy as it may be.

For me, that first night landing started out on "Cat 1." (The "cat" is the catapult mechanism designed to get your 45,000-pound airplane from 0 to 165 miles per hour in about 2 seconds.)

There I sat on Cat 1 with my knees shaking for what seemed like hours while waiting for the ground crew to finish its final checks on my aircraft.

When all the checks were complete, I ran the throttles to maximum power and gave a salute to the man who held my life in the balance with the catapult launch button.

He pushed the small green button that sent me propelling into the cloudy darkness off the San Diego coast.

My adventure had begun.

Some time, long ago, some Navy guy got the idea that it would be a solid idea to give pilots some extra time in the air in order to get *comfortable* before making their attempt at the carrier deck. Of course, what this guy failed to realize was that the entire time you are flying over a carrier, you are *far from comfortable*.

This guy probably got a medal while pilots everywhere spent 30 minutes in anxious anticipation of the inevitable, wondering, "Can we get this over with, please?!"

I spent my own comfort time trying to keep calm, cool, and collected, but of course I was a bundle of nerves.

It really was a beautiful night. The stars were out. The full moon was bright. Everything was quite nice. Well — almost everything. You see, starting at 700 feet above the water and ending at about 1,200 feet, there was a very thick cloud layer.

Normally, this layer would not be too much of a problem. I'd had hundreds of hours of training to teach me to fly through clouds just like this one. Only, on this particular night, the cloud layer would be the source of a significant problem for me.

As I lined myself up behind the USS John Stennis using the navigational aids in the F-18, I took one more look at the clouds.

"No problem," I thought. "I've been here before; just a simple descent on my glide slope final course and I will be out of this cloud in no time."

As I descended into the cloud layer 1,200 feet above the water, I was overcome with vertigo.

Let's play make believe for a moment. Pretend that you are standing blindfolded in the middle of a room and someone spins you around about 20 times, then just stops you cold. That dizzy, disoriented feeling is vertigo.

Normally, vertigo is just uncomfortable, but in a high-performance fighter it can be *deadly*.

On that first carrier landing approach, my brain started to lie to me. I felt a gentle rolling sensation to the left telling me to move the stick to the right to correct the airplane.

But just as I was about to turn right, I took a look at my Heads-Up-Display, which is the instrument that tells a pilot whether he is climbing, descending, turning right, or turning left. My instruments revealed the impossible:

I was flying straight and level!

All the while it felt like I was tumbling out of

control, in a death spiral to the left. My whole self was screaming, "Roll right! Roll right! You are going to crash!"

Just as I was about to turn the airplane to the right (which would have inevitably led to my death), I heard a small, still voice in the back of my head say,

"Trust your instruments."

The argument in my head may have only lasted a few seconds, but it felt like a lifetime. The whole time, I was positive that I was about to crash into the water at any moment.

"So, this is how it ends?" I thought.

That night, I had to choose from the following: trust myself or trust my instruments; trust my instincts or trust my *training*.

Webster's Dictionary defines vertigo as "a disordered state in which the individual or the individual's surroundings seem to whirl dizzily; a dizzy, confused state of mind."

I define it as the condition that nearly killed me.

Webster's defines training as "forming by instruction, discipline, or drill; to teach so as to make fit, qualified, or proficient."

I define it as the discipline that saved my life.

I listened to my training that night, and it made all the difference in the world. I landed successfully aboard the USS Stennis and rolled out of the landing area. My legs were shaking uncontrollably.

So much for being as cool as Iceman, huh?

I would like to tell you that the reason I am alive today is due to my quick thinking, my superior piloting skills, and my above-average intellect. I'd love to take credit for the work that I did that night and to pat myself on the back.

I cannot do that.

I must give credit where credit is due. I have a legacy to thank — over 100 years of aviation excellence passed from pilot to pilot, from instructor to student, until it reached me, when my own instructor said, "Ed, when all else fails, trust your instruments."

For those of us who must make life-changing decisions, I am fully convinced that the quality of those decisions is determined well before the day the decisions are made.

The decisions you will make tomorrow are based on the habits and the experience you have built throughout your life. In short, what you decide will be a function of who you are; and who you are will be a function of your training.

What decisions have you made this week?

Perhaps millions of dollars rested on a decision you made, or perhaps it was simply the dinner selection for your hungry children. In either case, you have been disciplined to make decisions based on your training, however formal or informal that training may have been.

The key, then, becomes molding and shaping

your influences to mold and shape you. My fate was finalized that night behind the carrier, but it wasn't decided then.

My fate had been decided months before when I spent hours flying a simulated airplane through simulated clouds onto a simulated carrier. My training saved my life that night.

So — how is YOUR training?

If you often feel overwhelmed by the challenges you face daily, let me encourage you to take time every day to train yourself. You can start with reading. I cannot remember a day in recent history when I did not spend some time reading. I personally read at least one book a week, and some times as many as four.

I personally start just about every day with 30 minutes of Bible reading, prayer, and meditation. I can't think of a better way to start a day. If you want to align every area of your life, start there.

But don't stop there. Read biographies of

successful people, read success literature, read inspirational books. You should read fiction too: It keeps your mind active and clears your head of the world for awhile.

Listen to audios and podcasts from seminars or trainings that apply to your work or passion. I download about 4 to 5 hours of material into my iPhone at the beginning of the week. Then I listen as I am working out, doing the dishes, driving to the post office, etc.

The number of ways to train yourself for success is endless.

The time to start is right now.

ACTION STEPS

---

1. Write down a list of the three books you are going to read this month. Commit to reading at least 30 minutes every day. Read with a pen and something to take notes on.

2. Commit to attending at least one seminar or training event for your specific interest, work, or hobby. If one is not available or the cost is too much, see if you can get the seminar (or one like it) on audio or video.

SECTION 3:

TRIGGER DOWN

How to fight and beat a MiG-29

SECTION 3:

TRIGGER DOWN

"Remember, people will judge you by your actions, not your intentions. You may have a heart of gold — but so does a hard-boiled egg."
- Anonymous

"To avoid criticism, do nothing, say nothing, and be nothing."
- Elbert Hubbard,
author of A Message to Garcia
(Note: Read it!)

The hands-down, number one dream of a lifetime for any F-18 fighter pilot is to fight against Russian-made MiG aircraft. And the only thing better than fighting one is to fight one and *win*.

I have done both.

But first, lest you think I am divulging some deeply hidden government secret about an air battle that "never happened" over some country that "doesn't exist," I should say that while the battle occurred between two real-life airplanes in real-life air, both of us were using simulated missiles. In other words, the loser did not actually blow up. The only thing at stake that day was bragging rights and a round at the bar.

What made things tough for me was that the German pilot flying the Russian-made MiG-29 Fulcrum was the commanding officer of the German squadron — and I was just a young pilot.

While he had almost 20 years under his belt, I had about two. Add to that the fact that his airplane had superior turn performance and better missiles. I was at a significant disadvantage.

My heart was pounding.

One-against-one fighter combat is like a chess match. Both pilots do their very best to make perfect decisions with perfect timing.

One pilot maneuvers; the other counters.

One pilot counters; the other maneuvers.

The key to winning this type of combat is to think *just* ahead of your opponent: to anticipate his move and react accordingly. While both pilots will likely make many small mistakes during the course of a dogfight, the pilot who emerges as the victor will be the one who minimizes his mistakes while capitalizing on his opponent's mistakes.

I'll share the story of what happened that day so you can imagine it in your mind's eye:

Imagine two airplanes flying directly at each other at about 850 miles an hour and then passing each other about 500 feet apart — not close enough to see the whites of our eyes, but pretty close nonetheless.

That's me in the "good guy" airplane. Here's what I am seeing. He turned into the vertical, so I did the same, both of us pulling over seven times our normal weight and struggling not to black out from turning so hard.

After we met again, we had both flown nearly flawless maneuvers, leaving us practically neutral at 22,000 feet above the ground.

"This is not going to be easy," I thought. "Just stay with the plan, fly smart, and don't make any mistakes."

Just as the MiG-29 passed down my left-hand side, I saw the pilot maneuver, leaving me a small window to counter and gain a much-desired offensive advantage.

It would be tough to explain just what he did wrong that day, but what I can say is that my window of opportunity would be open for about 3 seconds — after which it would snap shut and the chance would be lost.

Waiting for just the right moment, I quickly rolled my aircraft to the left using the fly-by-wire stick and rudders; then I pulled my nose to bear just in time to squeeze off a simulated missile.

Score one for the good guys. (I always star as the good guy in all of my stories BTW).

Then I slowly pivoted the airplane using the rudders to align my plane with his flight path. At just the right moment, I squeezed the trigger on hundreds of simulated 20mm bullets. They went flying through the air and into his airplane.

Mission success - game over.

I have often wondered why a young pilot in an inferior aircraft could have been so successful that day. In the end, I believe my keys to success can be summed up in two words:

Information and Implementation

For the two years leading up to that dogfight, I had been taught by some very capable pilots. Often they would create a scenario just like the one that led to my victory and teach me step by step how to counter a MiG-29.

That INFORMATION served me well. However, all by itself it still would have done me no good. IMPLEMENTATION was necessary.

I needed to see the MiG's mistake, recognize it, and counter it at just the right time. Then I needed to get my airplane in a position to shoot a missile and bullets — all without giving up my own advantage.

I did not win because I was better. I won because I had good information coupled with good implementation.

There are really only four types of people in the world. You can see them in the four quadrants on the next page.

	No Information	Information
No Implementation	Type 1	Type 2
Implementation	Type 3	Type 4

Type 1 — No Information/No Implementation

This is the proverbial couch potato. No need to feel sorry for this guy. His steady diet of reality TV, Home Shopping Network, food stamps, and government cheese is all his fault. He's either convinced himself that he is not capable of doing anything, or he is just too lazy to do it.

The Bible has the best instruction for dealing with this guy: "If a man will not work, he should not eat."

If you have gotten this far in the book, rest assured this is not you. But there is always a caution for all of us to avoid the temptation to be Type 1 lazy.

The key to avoiding this category is context: When you are working, work; when you are playing, play; and when you are relaxing, relax.

Type 2 — All Information/No Implementation

These are the know-it-alls who talk a big game, but never actually do anything. They are the ones who use the phrase, "I am going to..."

"I am going to write a book."

"I am going to quit my job and start my own business."

"I am going to ask her out on a date."

The problem is that they never get around to actually doing anything. And to make matters worse, when you do something, they are the first critics in line to tell you the way you should have done it.

To avoid this Type 2 trap, take action, then talk about what you did — not what you are going to do.

Type 3 — No Information/All Implementation

You have to feel sorry for these guys — they are chickens with their heads cut off. They go from one thing to the next, trying, trying, and trying harder. They just never get anywhere because they don't know what they are doing.

If only they would take a few minutes to get some advice, they'd be on their way to success. The problem is, they don't have time to ask — they're too busy doing.

I often picture this kind of person with his e-mail account open, Facebook notifications on, and his phone buzzing. You have to give him credit for doing something. It's just that in all his doing he never gets anything *done*.

To avoid this Type 3 trap, keep in mind that motion does not actually signify progress. Jogging in place may be good for warming up, but you will never finish the marathon unless you start moving forward.

Type 4 — All Information/All Implementation

This is the goal. Strive to be as educated as possible about everything and anything that you do—then do it! If you want to lose weight, study nutrition and diet plans, take a course on fitness, and then get busy.

If you want to start a business, take a few courses from some competent instructors, then get that Web page up and start making sales. If you want to learn how to be a gourmet cook, buy a few books, then get cooking, partner!

Any way you shake it, strive to be a Type 4 person. The spoils do not belong to the smart or to the strong—they belong to the one who first points in the right direction (information) and then runs (implementation).

Much like my dogfight with the MiG-29, we will all have the opportunities of a lifetime.

It could be a home-run sale or that job interview you've been waiting for. It could be a million-dollar merger or it could just be a line that's going to get you a date with the girl across the room.

In any case, the key to success is the same — coupling information with implementation.

The outcome of your chance of a lifetime is being decided *right now*. Whatever your goals may be, take the time to study and practice for that day, so when it does come, you will be able to squeeze the trigger on success.

ACTION STEPS

This chapter's action steps are simple:

1. Write down one goal. Make it short and sweet (e.g., learn to speed-read).

2. Take some time to attend a few courses or read some books on the topic.

3. Learn it!

4. Do it!

WHO IS IN CONTROL HERE ANYWAY?

Why you don't argue with a $40 million dollar jet

SECTION 4:

WHO IS IN CONTROL HERE ANYWAY?

"'Illusion of control' is the tendency for human beings to believe they can control, or at least influence, outcomes that they demonstrably have no influence over."
- Wikipedia

There are times in life when you just have to let go.

This is a lesson I learned while at the controls of an F-18 fighter. Yes, it is true — most pilots are control freaks. But there is one time in a fighter pilot's life when he cannot afford to do things his own way.

That time is when he is out of control.

Sound strange? Well, read on...

Do you remember in the movie *Top Gun* when Maverick was applauded for flying at the "edge of the envelope?"

Well, unlike our friend Maverick, most (sane) pilots strive to stay *inside* the envelope. Flying outside of the envelope means you no longer have control of your airplane. Flying out of the envelope is not flying, it's falling.

Case in point...

In the F-18, if you get going really fast, then

pull straight up, soon you will run out of speed and start coming back down again. Unfortunately, the coming-back-down part can be quite violent. The air usually flows over the back of the wings, then the side, then the back again. In other words, airplanes are meant to fly straight — and when they don't, they may never regain control again.

Pilots affectionately call this situation "OCF," short for "Out-of-Control Flight." And every fighter pilot (without exception) has a set of procedures that he must be able to recite and perform from rote memory.

He is tested on these procedures at least once a month and will not be permitted to fly if he fails to recite them perfectly from memory. In the case of the F-18, the OCF procedure is about six lines long and starts like this...

"Controls —release."

Can you believe that? The first thing you are supposed to do when the F-18 becomes uncontrollable is to release the controls!

In effect, this procedure boldly exclaims that the airplane is better at getting itself out of these difficult circumstances than the pilot. Of course, that's all well and good until you realize that the most difficult thing for your average control freak pilot to do is let go of anything.

But that is what the procedure says, and that is what we do.

Most pilots hope they never end up in an out of control airplane. And most are good enough to make that happen.

Not me.

I've been Out of Control twice. (Hooray for me.)

The last time I remember going out of control was over the ocean west of the Japanese island of Okinawa. It was during a one-against-one dogfight. I had a very junior wingman with me that day and I was going to teach him a thing or two about how to dogfight an F-18...

...or so I thought.

We met at a merge similar to the one in my dogfight with the MiG-29, and both airplanes went up. As we met again, I began to execute a maneuver that was bound to secure my victory.

Only this time, I misjudged both my altitude and my airspeed (bad combination).

And I soon found myself simultaneously out of airspeed and ideas (another bad combination).

For a brief minute, I tried to right the airplane using my own efforts. Then my training and rote memorization kicked in, and I began to execute the OCF procedure just as I had been taught.

- Controls — release

- Feet — off rudders

- Speed brake — in

- If still out of control —

    ○ Throttles — idle

- ○ Altitude, angle of attack, airspeed, and yaw rate — check

- When recovery indicated by angle of attack and yaw rate tones removed, side forces subsided, and airspeed accelerated above 180 knots — recover

The airplane bucked, then pitched up; the nose pushed down; and I was looking at a glare shield full of water. I was hurtling uncontrollably toward the ocean at a rate of 20,000 feet per minute. At my altitude, I knew that if the plane was not under control in less than 30 seconds, I would have to eject.

"Controls — release." I recited the procedure again in my head.

Then, as if my jet had been planning this all along and right at the last minute (literally), it started flying again.

As my airspeed increased, I put my right hand back on the stick and pulled the nose up toward the horizon - a very nervous (but very alive) pilot. A few minutes later, I was landing safe and sound on the runway back at our base.

Now...I'm not proud about almost losing an airplane. But I relearned some lessons that afternoon that I hope can help you.

First, I relearned the value of systems. I had my out-of-control flight system memorized verbatim, and it may have saved my life. In a jet, when you have 30 seconds until you must eject, there is no time to flip through a book to find the answer.

In the same way, systems can make or break your business or organization. For every decision that can be made in the boardroom, there are two that need to be made on the spot.

A good decision made now is better than a great decision made too late. And the key to timely decision making is good systems.

If the people in your organization know ahead of time what to decide when they are empowered to make decisions, they will be successful, and so will you.

Incidentally, one of the very first things I do with a new client is find ways that they can systematize their business (i.e. put it on autopilot). Who wants to run a company if it means you have to be there all of the time? That's what systems are for.

And once systems are in place, not only does the business usually explode in profits, but the owner normally starts taking some long vacations without his computer or cell phone.

Second, I learned that there are some times when you just have to *let go*.

In this case, the flight control computers in the F-18 were smarter (and faster) than the (mildly attractive) pilot who had gotten it into this mess.

The $40 million airplane knew better. So I let go, and it made all the difference in the world.

In the same way, as a leader in your

organization (or in your home), it's likely there are ways that you need to let go.

Is it possible that someone in your organization is better equipped to solve certain problems than you are?

Do you empower your people to solve problems — even if they are problems you have created?

Like many fighter pilots, leaders can soon become phenomenal control freaks. However, great leaders are not afraid to admit that sometimes they are not the right people to solve certain problems. Great leaders know when to let go.

Are things getting out of control? Whether it's $4 on the line or $40 million, the answer is simple:

Follow your systems and let go!

ACTION STEPS

---

1. Take some time to identify the number one request for information that you receive from (take your pick) employees, subordinates, or customers (e.g., "Tom, we just got a request for a refund; what do you want me to do?").

2. Using your response to that question, establish a system (e.g., "From now on, all refunds under $500 can be approved and processed by Jane.").

3. Empower those below you to act on your guidance (e.g., "Jane, you have been with me long enough to know how to deal with customer support issues like this. I trust you to make the right decision.").

SECTION 5:

KNOW YOUR PEOPLE AND LEAD WITH CONFIDENCE

SECTION 5:

KNOW YOUR PEOPLE AND LEAD WITH CONFIDENCE

"Leadership is the art of getting someone else to do something you want done because he wants to do it."
- Dwight D. Eisenhower

"I've sentenced boys younger than you to the gas chamber. Didn't want to do it — felt I owed it to them."
- Judge Smails, Caddyshack

It was so *cold*, wet, and rainy.

I was covered with grease, oil, and fuel. My fingers were numb (one was bleeding), and to top it all off, it was 1 a.m. and I needed to sleep.

Did I mention it was cold?

But even though I wasn't feeling all warm and fuzzy, *they* loved every minute of it — and I wouldn't have traded it for the world.

"They" happened to be a small group of mechanics ranging from 18 to 28 years old who were staying up all night to change an engine in an F-18.

"I" happened to be their leader. And, truth be told, I had been looking for an opportunity exactly like that.

In a typical Marine F-18 squadron, there are approximately 150 Marines who specialize in maintaining the unit's 12 airplanes. About 30 of them work on the engines.

These were my Marines, and having just recently been assigned to be their officer in charge, I was anxious for an opportunity to show them that I was a real person who actually cared for them.

Although I knew that particular night would be long and I would be flying the next day, I purposely exchanged my good night's sleep to spend it with my men, helping them change the engine. And while they did not need my help, what they did need was to know that their boss cared about them.

That night, I gave them my time, and in turn, they gave me their trust. As the hours went by, one by one, the men started telling me their problems. From marital difficulties to credit card overages; from sick kids to annoying girlfriends, I heard them all.

Then and only then was I able to guide them as a true leader — one who truly knew his men.

Perhaps you can relate to my story. You have

people that are under your leadership, and you realize that you don't know what makes them tick. Perhaps you have someone who works right next to you, and you don't even know what his wife's name is.

A simple method for taking your leadership from normal to dynamic is to know your people. The following three steps could change forever the way your people follow you:

1. Get dirty. For me, getting dirty was literal. For you, getting dirty may be as simple as asking your colleague how her husband's birthday party was or what she gave her son for Christmas.

2. Ask questions. These include, but are not limited to, family names, interests, hobbies, etc. Be creative here, but avoid the obvious. For example, my dad used to be an NBA referee. About four times a day, someone would ask him if he'd ever met Michael Jordan. That gets old quickly. Before you

start asking questions, think about the obvious ones and reject them if necessary.

3. Write down your findings. When I was in charge of our engine mechanics, I kept a binder in which I kept track of our discussions. I would occasionally use this log to refresh my memory. So, for example, when I went up to Corporal Jones three months after our last discussion and asked him how his wife Jennifer was doing with her pregnancy, it gave him the distinct impression that I cared about him, and I did.

Knowing your people is a skill that takes time and dedication, but it can make the difference between being the kind of leader whose motto is "Follow me!" and the kind whose motto is "I'm their leader—which way did they go?"

One thing is certain: You are a leader. It doesn't matter if you are the CEO of a Fortune 500 company or the mother of two, the guy who started Apple or the guy who starts the wave at the next ball game; people are looking to you for guidance.

Oftentimes, the difference between dynamic leaders and poor ones is simply how well they know and care for their people.

Of course, as you look for opportunities to lead from the front, a word of caution is in order: Do not be like the boss who took all the bolts off his door and announced an "open door policy" for all employees. If you do that, you are asking for every cook and bottle washer to steal every minute out of every day with their minute problems.

"Do you have a second?" is really code for, "Can I suck away all of your time like a vampire sucks blood?"

"Tom, do you think this looks best in red or blue?"

"Hi Bill, listen, can I pick your brain for a few minutes about the Nelson account?"

Don't let that happen to you. The most important thing your subordinates need is for you to be productive.

And when you do set solid guidelines regarding your time, they will be all the happier when you take a few minutes to get dirty and ask specific and meaningful questions.

ACTION STEPS

1. Find at least one way every day to get "dirty" and do it.

2. At least once a week, write down some information about an employee, friend, or co-worker that you can use later (e.g., "Hi Bill, last week you mentioned you we're going to your son's soccer tournament. How did that go?").

SECTION 6:

FOCUS ON THE TARGET AND PLAN BACKWARD

The fighter pilot key to mission success

SECTION 6:

FOCUS ON THE TARGET AND PLAN BACKWARD

"The reason most people never reach their goals is that they don't define them, or ever seriously consider them as believable or achievable. Winners can tell you where they are going, what they plan to do along the way, and who will be sharing the adventure with them."

- Dr. Denis Waitley, author of The Psychology of Winning

"If you don't know where you are going, any road will take you there."

- Lewis Carroll, Alice in Wonderland

The more things change, the more they remain the same. Compared to the small, single-engine biplanes that the U.S. military flew in World War I, today's combat fighters are sleek, stealthy, and capable of raining destruction upon the enemy at great ranges.

But while technology has changed a great deal over the past 80+ years, combat missions themselves have not changed much at all. To put it simply, just about every mission can be summarized as follows:

1. Fight your way to the target.

2. Drop your bombs.

3. Fight your way home.

The rest is just the icing on the cake.

Armed with that knowledge, one of my keys to properly planning a mission over enemy territory has been to focus on the target and work backward.

In other words, I typically prioritize my planning around the reason I am going into harm's way in the first place: to take out a target.

It would make no sense to get airborne, shoot down a few MiGs, and dodge some surface-to-air fire just for the sheer thrill value (although it does sound fun).

"Starting at the target" means that I take a good look at the target's strengths and weaknesses. The process involves planning what ordnance would have the best effect on the target, investigating the best axis from which to attack, and planning the best flight formation to accomplish the task. Only once that is complete, do I plan the rest of the flight.

The more I write about the subject of personal productivity and leadership, the more I realize how many of the things I have learned in the cockpit of the F-18 transfer directly into the real world.

This subject is no exception. The principle of starting at the target and working backward can be an invaluable (and money-making) tool for you and your company. The process itself is so simple that it can easily get lost in the shuffle. Here it is:

1. Describe the target.

In order to reach your goals, you need to have some. That may sound obvious, but you'd be surprised at how many people miss this step. Your goal or mission should be able to fit on the back of a business card.

An example of a good mission-oriented goal starts with the phrase, "My final desired result is..."

Military example — "My final desired result is the complete destruction of the enemy airfield storage shelters."

Business example — "My final desired result is a 30% increase in online advertising efficiency as determined by an increase in our click-through rate from 3% to 4% over the next month."

2. Describe the actions necessary to reach the target.

This is the time to peel back the onion and assign detailed tasks and deliverables to each of your subordinate leaders. Take a four-step approach:

Task

Purpose

Method

End State

a. Task

This is the step you want your subordinate to take.

Task: Split-test two ads online.

b. Purpose

This is why you are doing something. It gives a direction that can be followed in your absence. It usually begins with the phrase, "In order to..."

Purpose: In order to increase overall ad

effectiveness on all keywords.

c.   Method

The devil is in the details, and this is where you put the meat on the bones of a good mission. Fill in anything that needs to be filled in to answer the question, "How?" And by all means, don't be like most people and assume that everyone can read your mind.

How: Using Google AdWords and only on the search network (not on content sites).

d.   End State

This is where you communicate your goal from step one. It starts with, "My final desired result is..."

End state: My final desired result is a 30% increase in online advertising efficiency as determined by an increase in our click-through rate from 3% to 4% over the next month.

Here is what the entire mission statement

sounds like:

Split-test two ads online in order to increase overall ad effectiveness on all keywords using Google AdWords and only on the search network (not on content sites). My final desired result is a 30% increase in online advertising efficiency as determined by an increase in our click-through rate from 3% to 4% over the next month.

Some more examples:

Rework the Johnson proposal [TASK] in order to wrap up all the loose ends we have identified [PURPOSE] using the planning matrix from page 39 of the manual [METHOD]. My final desired result is a complete and edited proposal on my desk by 3 p.m. on Friday [END STATE].

Write an FAQ page on the Web site [TASK] in order to help reduce customer service calls on basic questions [PURPOSE]. You can have Jim and Phil from the call center for two hours tomorrow afternoon [METHOD]. My final desired result is a comprehensive FAQ page posted to the site by close of business tomorrow afternoon [END STATE].

3. Conduct Concurrent Planning.

For larger projects, allow your subordinates time to do their own mission analysis and tasking (steps 1 and 2). Be sure to give them tight deadlines. Remember that tasks expand if given too much time.

4. Supervise.

This critical step is not to be confused with micromanagement. This is where you hold all of your people accountable for reaching their goals and deadlines without looking over their shoulders.

Repeat this process periodically for each of your missions.

Finally, remember that this process does not require any more meetings. It requires action.

Try focusing on the target and working backward on your next task. I think you'll see unparalleled mission success.

Action Steps

---

1. Write down a difficult task (i.e., one that you normally do yourself because no one else could possibly get it right).

2. Delegate that task using Task, Purpose, Method, and End State (be sure to establish a deadline), and see how much it improves performance.

SECTION 7:

THE GENERAL WANTS TO SEE YOU

How to think on your feet when you're in front of the boss

SECTION 7:

THE GENERAL WANTS
TO SEE YOU

"I know you've heard it a thousand times before. But it's true — hard work pays off. If you want to be good, you have to practice, practice, practice. If you don't love something, then don't do it."

- Ray Bradbury

Recently, I got an e-mail that read like this: "You have an appointment Tuesday morning to meet with General Jones" (name changed to protect the guilty, er, I mean the innocent).

That was the entire text of the message.

There was no explanation, no topic, no "cordially invited" — just a date and time.

Has that ever happened to you? It was probably not a Marine Corps general who summoned you into his presence, but have you ever been sitting at your desk, minding your own business, when the phone rings with a message that the boss wants to see you?

I don't know about you, but my mind immediately goes to the worst possible scenario. ("That's it! I'm going to jail.")

In case you ever find yourself in that situation - especially when you're nervous, here is a valuable tool to help you hit a home run in front of the boss, every time:

Do some "chair-flying."

Chair-flying is a fighter pilot term for pre-flight practice.

Most pilots, at some time in their careers, master the art of flying an entire sortie at their desks before they ever get to an airplane. When a pilot chair-flies, he makes radio calls, deals with emergencies, and dodges hostile fire — all while sitting at his desk with his eyes closed. It is a way to build some much-needed experience even before he's got it.

And it really works.

The following example is for those who have an actual boss. For those who don't, the concepts below work equally well for partners, clients, customers, or patients. In fact, they even work when you're not there; some of the best sales letters I have ever written follow these five steps.

When you get the call to the corner office, spend a minute to chair-fly your way through the meeting. When you do, follow this simple but powerful checklist:

1. Briefly put yourself in the boss's mind. What does he (or she) want to know? What is he going to ask? How is he going to ask it? Write each question or concern down on a piece of paper or an index card.

2. Come up with a well-worded, clear, and short answer to each of the anticipated questions. Write the answer to each question on the back of the card. Try to write each answer in the form of a benefit statement. These usually start with, "What this means to you is…"

3. Go through your answers as if you were in the boss's office. There is no need, nor is there time, for memorization; just practice them once or twice in your head, and they will be guaranteed to come out much clearer in real life.

4. In your live responses, be sure to state

your boss's likely objections — and then answer them.

Example: "Tom, at first glance, it may seem like we are not going to get the return back from this investment that we normally do [OBJECTION].

"However, thinking long-term, this is a deal that will require a small investment now and should return thousands over the next 10 years [ANSWER]."

5. Finally, close strong. Failing to close strong is one of the biggest mistakes you can make when talking to your boss, especially when you are thinking on your feet.

For some reason, we all clam up when it comes to the big ending. (This is equally true for salesmen asking for the sale, copywriters writing the offer, contractors asking for payment, and guys asking for a date.) And the higher the boss's position, the worse it usually gets.

But think about it from your boss's

perspective. He wants his employees to be assertive and strong. Trust me on this.

Understanding this principle alone could get you your next promotion. To close strong, end with something like, "Finally, unless we are willing to give up a significant market share, we have little choice but to proceed with this purchase."

So the next time you are called to the boss's office, do a little chair-flying ahead of time and ensure your success.

ACTION STEPS

---

1. Identify one thing this last month that took you off guard.

2. Write down two things you could have done to prevent that from happening.

3. Next, identify something else that could take you off guard that hasn't happened yet.

4. Come up with a short contingency plan for that possibility.

SECTION 8:

WHAT TO DO NEXT

How to Break into The

Top 20% and Achieve

Your Dreams

WHAT TO DO NEXT

"It's not a great ideas until it is a great idea implemented"
- Ed Rush
(Yes, I quoted myself. :))

Congrats!

You've made it to the end of this book. Seriously, I am not patronizing you. You are now in the 20% of people who finish what they start. Maybe I'm being optimistic. It's probably more like 5%.

That is a great step in the right direction.

Now that you are here, you've got one last thing to do. Take your action items and do them! Be sure to set a deadline for each one; otherwise they won't get done.

If you're interested in having me come in and speak or consult for your company, (not so subtle pitch coming here) then shoot me an email or head on over to...

www.EdRush.com

Finally, if you enjoyed the stories and principles in this book, why not get some books for your employees, co-workers, clients, friends, family, kids, and relatives?

And be sure to let me hear your success story!

I'd love to hear how you are implementing the strategies you've learned here.

Made in the USA
San Bernardino, CA
06 April 2016